Editor
Gisela Lee, M.A.

Managing Editor
Karen Goldfluss, M.S. Ed.

Editor-in-Chief
Sharon Coan, M.S. Ed.

Cover Artist
Barb Lorseyedi

Art Coordinator
Kevin Barnes

Art Director
CJae Froshay

Imaging
Rosa C. See

Product Manager
Phil Garcia

Publishers
Rachelle Cracchiolo, M.S. Ed.
Mary Dupuy Smith, M.S. Ed.

Practice Makes Perfect

Math Brain Teasers

GRADE 5

Author

Mary Rosenberg

Teacher Created Materials, Inc.
6421 Industry Way
Westminster, CA 92683
www.teachercreated.com

ISBN-0-7439-3755-4

©2003 Teacher Created Materials, Inc.
Made in U.S.A.

Table of Contents

Introduction. 3

Brain Teaser 1: Brain Puzzlers (word problems) 4

Brain Teaser 2: Broken Eggs (logic and reasoning) 6

Brain Teaser 3: Numbers (logic and reasoning) 7

Brain Teaser 4: A Canine Question (graphing) 8

Brain Teaser 5: Phone Numbers (logic and reasoning). 10

Brain Teaser 6: Grades (logic and reasoning) 11

Brain Teaser 7: Paper Routes (logic and reasoning) 12

Brain Teaser 8: Great Googols (exponential numbers). 13

Brain Teaser 9: Pascal's Triangle (number patterns). 15

Brain Teaser 10: Fastest Feet (time) 18

Brain Teaser 11: Arts and Crafts (time). 19

Brain Teaser 12: Graphing Functions (graphing) 20

Brain Teaser 13: A Famous Landmark (integers) 21

Brain Teaser 14: Math Squares #1 (mixed practice). 22

Brain Teaser 15: Math Squares #2 (mixed practice). 23

Brain Teaser 16: Get into Shape! (geometry) 24

Brain Teaser 17: Number Puzzle #1 (math puzzles). 25

Brain Teaser 18: Number Puzzle #2 (math puzzles). 26

Brain Teaser 19: Number Puzzle #3 (math puzzles). 27

Brain Teaser 20: Number Puzzle #4 (math puzzles). 28

Brain Teaser 21: Simple Sequences (sequences). 29

Brain Teaser 22: Harder Sequences (sequences). 30

Brain Teaser 23: Fibonacci Sequence (sequences) 31

Brain Teaser 24: Coin Combinations Less Than a Dollar (money) 32

Brain Teaser 25: Coin Combinations More Than a Dollar (money). 33

Brain Teaser 26: Coin Combinations and Dollar Bills (money). 34

Brain Teaser 27: A Roll of the Dice #1 (mixed practice) 35

Brain Teaser 28: A Roll of the Dice #2 (mixed practice) 36

Brain Teaser 29: Who's the Smartest? (using logical reasoning and charts) 37

Brain Teaser 30: Logic Problems and Charts (using logical reasoning and charts). 39

Brain Teaser 31: TV Channels (mixed practice). 41

Brain Teaser 32: Number Teaser #1 (logic and reasoning). 42

Brain Teaser 33: Number Teaser #2 (logic and reasoning). 43

Brain Teaser 34: Number Puzzle 24 (logic and reasoning). 44

Brain Teaser 35: Name the President (money) 45

Answer Key 46

Introduction

The old adage "practice makes perfect" can really hold true for your child and his or her education. The more practice and exposure your child has with concepts being taught in school, the more success he or she is likely to find. For many parents, knowing how to help your children can be frustrating because the resources may not be readily available. As a parent it is also difficult to know where to focus your efforts so that the extra practice your child receives at home supports what he or she is learning in school.

This book has been designed to help parents and teachers reinforce basic skills with children. *Practice Makes Perfect* reviews basic math skills for children in grade 5. This book contains 35 brain teasers that allow children to learn, review, and reinforce math concepts. Brain teasers have long proved their worth as vehicles of learning. Such activities carry with them curiosity and delight. While it would be impossible to include all concepts taught in grade 5 in this book, the following basic objectives are reinforced through the brain teasers:

- word problems
- logic and reasoning
- graphing
- number patterns/sequences
- exponential numbers and integers

- time
- money
- basic geometry
- using charts and other graphics

How to Make the Most of This Book

Here are some useful ideas for optimizing the activity pages in this book:

- Set aside a specific place in your home to work on the activity pages. Keep it neat and tidy with materials on hand.

- Set up a certain time of day to work on the brain teasers. This will establish consistency. Look for times in your day or week that are less hectic and more conducive to practicing skills.

- Keep all practice sessions with your child positive and constructive.

- Help with instructions, if necessary. If your child is having difficulty understanding what to do or how to get started, work through the first problem with him or her.

- Review the work your child has done. This serves as reinforcement and provides further practice.

- Allow your child to use whatever writing instruments he or she prefers. For example, colored pencils can add variety and pleasure to the activity page.

- Pay attention to the areas that your child has the most difficulty. Provide extra guidance and exercises in those areas.

- Look for ways to make real-life applications to the skills being reinforced.

Brain Teaser 1 ♪ ☙ ♪ ♪ ☙ ♪ ♪ ☙ ♪ ♪ ☙ ♪ ♪ ☙

Brain Puzzlers

Directions: Solve these challenging brain teasers.

1. Tony saved *d* dollars in January. In February, he saved $5 more than he saved in January.

   (a) Write an expression that represents the number of dollars he saved in February.

   _____

   (b) Write an expression that represents the total number of dollars he saved in two months.

   _____

2. The length of a rectangle is four feet more than the width. Let *w* be the number of feet in the width. Then (*w* + 4) is the number of feet in the length. Write equations for the following:

   (a) The width when doubled is the same as the length increased by three.

   _____

   (b) Assume the length doubled is equal to the product of 3 and the width increased by 1.

   _____

   (c) Twice the width added to twice the length is equal to 36. (This is the perimeter of the rectangle.) _____

3. In shop class Don cut a 50-inch board into two pieces. One piece is 10 inches longer than the other piece. Find the length of the shorter piece. _____

4. In a class election, Ian received 5 more votes than Libbie. How many votes did Ian receive if all 35 students in the class voted? _____

5. If a number is added to twice the same number, the sum is less than 27. For what numbers greater than zero is this true? _____

6. The sum of three consecutive whole numbers is 123. What are the three numbers?

   _____

7. Mr. O'Leary is 4 times as old as his son. In 16 years he will be only twice as old. What are their ages now? (*Hint:* If the son is *x* years old now, how old will he be in another 16 years?)

   _____

8. Mary is 14 years old. She is five years older than her brother. How old is Mary's brother?

   _____

9. A boy is four years younger than his sister. If the boy is 10 years old, how old is his sister?

   _____

10. A boy's age seven years from now will be 20. How old is the boy now?

   _____

Brain Teaser 1 *(cont.)* ❧ ᕲ ❧ ᕲ ❧ ᕲ ❧ ᕲ ᕲ ❧

Brain Puzzlers *(cont.)*

11. Anne was 3 years old ten years ago. How old is Anne at the present time? _____

12. If one is added to twice a girl's age, the result is 19. What is the girl's age _____

13. Gloria had $40.00 in savings. Her mother gave her another $30.00 and her grandmother gave her $10.00 to buy a pair of running shoes. The pair of running shoes Gloria wants cost $54.99, tax included. Write an equation using a variable to describe the amount of money that Gloria will have to contribute from her savings to buy the shoes. Then solve the equation.

    _____

14. Uncle Henry grew 252 kilograms of cherries. He sold them to a grocer who divided them into 5-kg and 2-kg bags. If the grocer uses the same number of 5-kg bags as 2-kg bags, then how many bags did the grocer use in all? _____

15. An 800-seat multiplex is divided into 3 theatres. There are 270 seats in Theatre 1, and there are 150 more seats in Theatre 2 than in Theatre 3. How many seats are in Theatre 2? (*Hint:* Let x = number of seats in Theatre 3; T1 = Theatre 1 = 270 seats; T2 = Theatre 2 = 150 + x; T1 + T2 + T3 = 800 seats.) _____

16. The sum of 13 and twice a number is 75. Find the number. _____

17. Manuel has a board 16 feet long. He needs to cut it so that one piece is 1 foot longer than twice the length of the other. (*Hint:* If x = the length of the short board, then $2x + 1$ = the length of the longer board.) What will be the length of each board? _____

18. The sum of three consecutive integers is 69. What are the numbers? (*Hint:* Let x = the smallest number, $x + 1$ = the next smallest number, and $(x + 1) + 1$ or $x + 2$ = the third number.)

    _____

19. April wants her house to be a pale yellow. Pale yellow paint is made by mixing paint in a ratio of 9 parts white to 2 parts yellow. How much of each color is needed to make 22 gallons of pale yellow paint? _____

20. Margo sells perfume at the Smith and Jones department store. She makes $8.00 an hour and 15% commission on any bottle of perfume she sells. She works 8 hours a day. If each bottle of perfume costs $50 and she earned $470 in 5 days, how many bottles of perfume did she sell?

    _____

Brain Teaser 2

Broken Eggs

Each store owner ordered one gross (144) of eggs. Unfortunately, many of the eggs were cracked or broken! How many cracked or broken eggs did each store owner receive?

Read each clue. If the answer is "yes" make an "O" in the box. If the answer is "no" make an "X" in the box.

		9	18	36	72
Brenda					
Casey					
Daniel					
Eden					

Clues

1. Brenda received a number of broken eggs that is evenly divisible by 12.

2. Casey received a squared number of broken eggs.

3. Daniel received an odd number of broken eggs.

Brenda received _____ cracked or broken eggs.

Casey received _____ cracked or broken eggs.

Daniel received _____ cracked or broken eggs.

Eden received _____ cracked or broken eggs

Brain Teaser 3

Numbers

Read each clue. If the answer is "yes" make an "O" in the box. If the answer is "no" make an "X" in the box.

		25	31	34	71	84
Connor						
Hannah						
Logan						
Stan						
Tara						

Clues

1. Hannah only likes prime numbers.
2. Logan only likes numbers that have been squared.
3. Connor only likes number with all odd digits.
4. Tara only likes numbers larger than 7^2.
5. Connor's number is less than half the value of Hannah's number.

 Connor's number is _____.   Stan's number is _____.

 Hannah's number is _____.   Tara's number is _____.

 Logan's number is _____.

Brain Teaser 4

A Canine Question

Directions: Solve each system of equations below and on page 9 by graphing them. Using the solution, find the letter in the table on page 9 which matches the solution for each problem. Write this letter on the blank space which is labeled with the problem number. The resulting message will be the answer to the riddle.

1. $y = 3x$
   $y = \frac{1}{3}x$
   (,   )
   solution

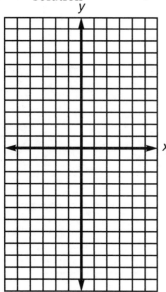

2. $x = -5$
   $y = x + -3$
   (,   )
   solution

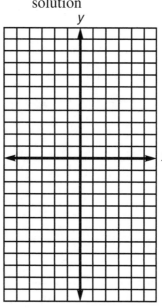

3. $y = -x$
   $y = 3x + 4$
   (,   )
   solution

4. $y = x + 4$
   $y = 2x + 5$
   (,   )
   solution

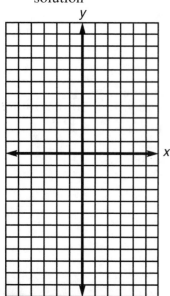

5. $y = 2x$
   $y = 3x - 3$
   (,   )
   solution

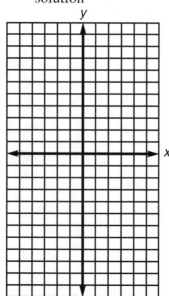

6. $x = 4$
   $y = -2$
   (,   )
   solution

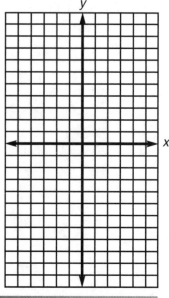

Brain Teaser 4 *(cont.)*

A Canine Question *(cont.)*

7. $y = 4 + 2x$
   $y - x = 4$
   (,)
   solution

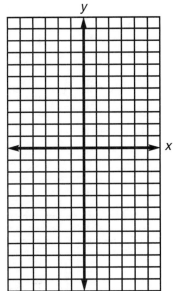

8. $y = 5x$
   $y = x + 4$
   (,)
   solution

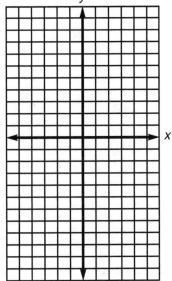

9. $y - 2x = 3$
   $y = x + 3$
   (,)
   solution

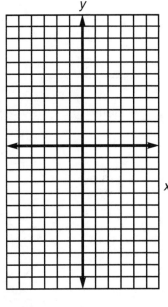

10. $y - 2x = 1$
    $y - x = -1$
    (,)
    solution

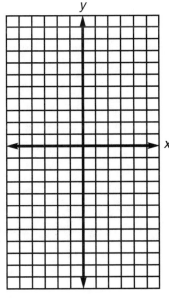

A (-1, -5)
B (0, 3)
C (1, 5)
D (-1, 1)
E (-3, -2)
F (10, 6)
G (-5, -8)
H (5, 10)
I (0, 0)
L (9, 4)
M (-4, -9)

N (-1, 3)
O (8, 4)
P (3, 9)
R (-1, 6)
S (3, 6)
T (1, 2)
U (0, 4)
V (4, -2)
W (6, 1)
Y (-2, -3)

Question: What is it called when a cartoon dog plunges into the water?

$\overline{}\ \overline{}\ \overline{}\ \overline{}\ \overline{}$
5   8   7   9   10

$\overline{}\ \overline{}\ \overline{}\ \overline{}\ \overline{}\ \overline{}$
3   1   6   1   4   2

Brain Teaser 5

Phone Numbers

Read each clue. If the answer is "yes" make an "O" in the box. If the answer is "no" make an "X" in the box.

		318-1041	528-6321	796-9934	837-2107	844-1109
Bella						
Destiny						
Ky						
Kendra						
Ryder						

Clues

1. Bella's and Ky's phone numbers both begin with the same digit.

2. When the digits are added together, both Ky and Ryder's phone numbers are of the same value.

3. Destiny's phone number has more odd than even digits.

 Bella's number is _____.   Ky's number is _____.

 Destiny's number is _____.   Kendra's number is _____.

 Ryder's number is _____.

Brain Teaser 6

Grades

Read each clue. If the answer is "yes" make an "O" in the box. If the answer is "no" make an "X" in the box.

		50%	55%	75%	80%	85%	100%
Andrew							
Brian							
Charles							
Emily							
Molly							
Sheila							

Clues

1. Sheila's score was 20 points higher than Brian's score.
2. Andrew's score was 20 points higher than Emily's score.
3. Charles did not answer half of the questions correctly.
4. Sheila's score was higher than Andrew's score.

 Andrew's score was _____.   Emily's score was _____.

 Brian's score was _____.   Molly's score was _____.

 Charles's score was _____.   Sheila's score was _____.

Brain Teaser 7

Paper Routes

Read each clue. If the answer is "yes" make an "O" in the box. If the answer is "no" make an "X" in the box.

	Camelot Park	Hyde park	Park Place	Park West	391	547	1,062	1,079
Bud								
Helen								
Jodie								
Nick								

Clues

1. Jodie delivers an odd number of newspapers to the residents of Park Place.
2. Camelot Park does not receive the most or the fewest number of newspapers.
3. Bud delivers papers to the residents of Park West.
4. Helen delivers the most newspapers.
5. Jodie delivers more newspapers than Bud.

Bud delivers _____ newspapers to the residents of _____.

Helen delivers _____ newspapers to the residents of _____.

Nick delivers _____ newspapers to the residents of _____.

Jodie delivers _____ newspapers to the residents of _____.

Brain Teaser 8 ꙮ ꙮ ꙮ ꙮ ꙮ ꙮ ꙮ ꙮ ꙮ ꙮ ꙮ

Great Googols

Number Names and Exponents

Extremely large numbers are often written with exponents to express their value. The names and values of large numbers are shown here as expressed in digits, with the written name and in exponential form.

$$1{,}000{,}000 \quad 1 \text{ million} \quad 10^{6}$$
$$1{,}000{,}000{,}000 \quad 1 \text{ billion} \quad 10^{9}$$
$$1{,}000{,}000{,}000{,}000 \quad 1 \text{ trillion} \quad 10^{12}$$
$$1{,}000{,}000{,}000{,}000{,}000 \quad 1 \text{ quadrillion} \quad 10^{15}$$
$$1{,}000{,}000{,}000{,}000{,}000{,}000 \quad 1 \text{ quintillion} \quad 10^{18}$$
$$1{,}000{,}000{,}000{,}000{,}000{,}000{,}000 \quad 1 \text{ sextillion} \quad 10^{21}$$
$$1{,}000{,}000{,}000{,}000{,}000{,}000{,}000{,}000 \quad 1 \text{ septillion} \quad 10^{24}$$
$$1{,}000{,}000{,}000{,}000{,}000{,}000{,}000{,}000{,}000 \quad 1 \text{ octillion} \quad 10^{27}$$
$$1{,}000{,}000{,}000{,}000{,}000{,}000{,}000{,}000{,}000{,}000 \quad 1 \text{ nonillion} \quad 10^{30}$$
$$1{,}000{,}000{,}000{,}000{,}000{,}000{,}000{,}000{,}000{,}000{,}000 \quad 1 \text{ decillion} \quad 10^{33}$$

Even Larger Names

$1 \text{ undecillion} = 10^{36}$ $1 \text{ duodecillion} = 10^{39}$

$1 \text{ tredecillion} = 10^{42}$ $1 \text{ quattuordecillion} = 10^{45}$

$1 \text{ quindecillion} = 10^{48}$ $1 \text{ sexdecillion} = 10^{51}$

$1 \text{ septendecillion} = 10^{54}$ $1 \text{ octodecillion} = 10^{57}$

$1 \text{ novemdecillion} = 10^{60}$ $1 \text{ vigintillion} = 10^{63}$

Great Googols

A *googol* is the name of a special number. It was created by the nine-year-old nephew of a mathematician. It represents a 1 followed by 100 zeros. It is written:

10,000,000,000,000,000,000,000,000,000,000,000,000,000,000,000,000,000,000,000,000,000,000,000,0
00,000,000,000,000,000,000,000,000

or

$$10^{100}$$

An even larger number is a *googolplex*. A googolplex is a googol times itself. It was invented by the same child. A googolplex is written:

$$10^{\text{gogool}} \quad \text{or} \quad \text{as an exponent: } 10^{100^{100}}$$

Brain Teaser 8 (cont.)

Great Googols (cont.)

Multiplying with Large Numbers

> Look at the following information:
> • A billion is 1,000 times a million.
> • A trillion is 1,000 times a billion.
> • A trillion is 1,000,000 times a million.

Directions: Study the information at the top of the page and on page 13 to help you answer the questions below.

1. What number is 1,000 times a billion? _____

2. What number is 1,000 times a trillion? _____

3. What number is 1,000 times a quadrillion? _____

4. What number is 1,000 times a quintillion? _____

5. What number is 1,000 times a sextillion? _____

6. What number is 1,000 times a septillion? _____

7. What number is 1,000,000 times a million? _____

8. What number is 1,000,000 times a billion? _____

9. What number is 1,000,000 times a trillion? _____

10. What number is 1,000,000 times a quadrillion? _____

11. 1,000,000,000
        x 1,000
     _____

12. 1,000,000,000,000
            x 1,000
     _____

13. 1,000,000,000,000
         x 1,000,000
     _____

14. 1,000,000,000,000
        x 1,000,000,000
     _____

15.   1,000,000
        x 1,000,000
     _____

16.   1,000,000,000
       x 1,000,000,000
     _____

17. What number is 1,000 times 1,000 times 1,000?

    1,000 x 1,000 x 1,000 = _____

18. What number is 1,000 times 1,000 times 1,000 times 1,000?

    1,000 x 1,000 x 1,000 x 1,000 = _____

19. 5,000,000,000 x 5,000,000 = _____

20. 9,000,000,000 x 9,000,000,000 = _____

Brain Teaser 9

Pascal's Triangle

Pascal's Triangle

One of the most famous number patterns in math is *Pascal's Triangle*. This patterned sequence can be used to predict the probability of an event. Study the pattern shown here in this triangular shape. Try to discover the pattern.

```
                    1
                 1     1
              1     2     1
           1     3     3     1
        1     4     6     4     1
     1     5    10    10     5     1
  1     6    15    20    15     6     1
1     7    21    35    35    21     7     1
___  ___  ___  ___  ___  ___  ___  ___  ___
```

Patterns

Look for these patterns:

- The number 1 is at the beginning and end of each row.
- The numbers, in counting order, descend as you move upward along the sides of the triangle next to the exterior 1s.
- The third set of numbers on each side are triangular numbers: 1, 3, 6, 10, 15, 21, etc.
- The center numbers in the triangle alternate between a single number, such as 6 and 20, and doubled numbers, such as 10 and 35.

Upside-down Triangles

You can draw a series of upside-down triangles connecting the numbers on Pascal's Triangle. The number at the bottom tip of the triangle is the sum of the two numbers at the upper points of the triangle. Look at the example below. This triangular pattern makes it possible to find the next row in Pascal's triangle.

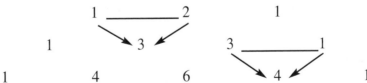

Doubling Totals

Add the total of each row across the triangle.

```
              1                                    1 =  1
           1     1                              1 + 1 =  2
        1     2     1                       1 + 2 + 1 =  4
     1     3     3     1                 1 + 3 + 3 + 1 =  8
  1     4     6     4     1          1 + 4 + 6 + 4 + 1 = 16
```

Each total is double the row above it.

Brain Teaser 9 *(cont.)*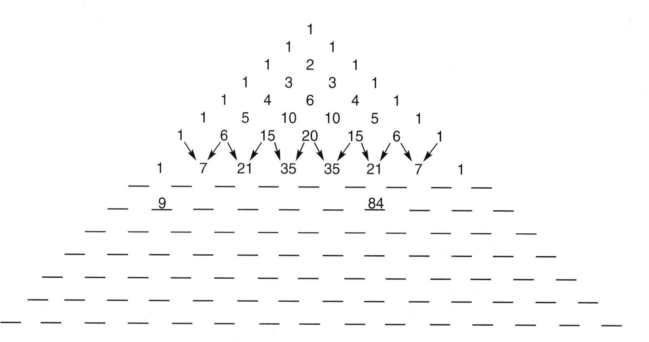

Pascal's Triangle *(cont.)*

Upside-down Triangles

Directions: Study the information on page 15. Draw upside-down triangles to show how the lower totals are computed. The first ones are done for you. Use this method to compute the missing numbers on the lower rows.

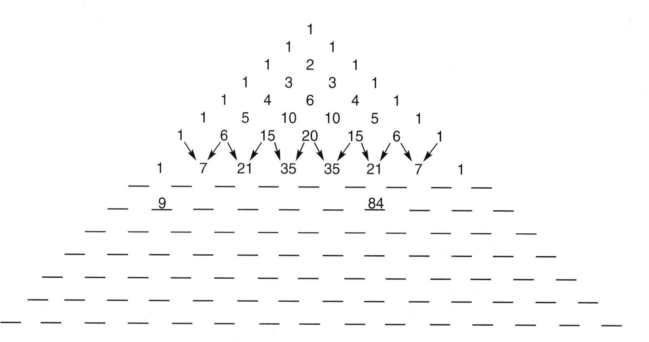

- The 1 at the top of the triangle is considered Row 0.
- The two 1s are Row 1.
- The triangle above shows Rows 0 through 14.

Directions: Study the information above and on the previous page. Then answer these questions. Use a calculator where needed.

1. Write the center number or numbers for the following rows:

   Row 9 _____   Row 11 _____   Row 13 _____

   Row 10 _____   Row 12 _____   Row 14 _____

2. What number is on the outside of every row? _____

3. Where on the triangle is the number indicating Rows 1 through 14? _____

4. Continue the triangular pattern for Row 15.

_____

Brain Teaser 9 (cont.)

Pascal's Triangle (cont.)

Working with Pascal's Triangle

Directions: Add the numbers in each row of the triangle and write the totals on the lines to the right of each row.

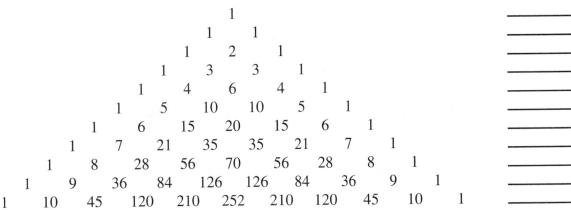

```
                          1                           _____
                       1     1                        _____
                    1     2     1                     _____
                 1     3     3     1                  _____
              1     4     6     4     1               _____
           1     5    10    10     5     1            _____
        1     6    15    20    15     6     1         _____
     1     7    21    35    35    21     7     1      _____
  1     8    28    56    70    56    28     8     1   _____
1     9    36    84   126   126    84    36     9     1   _____
1    10    45   120   210   252   210   120    45    10     1   _____
```

How does the total of each row relate to the row above it?

_____

Directions: Study the information on page 15. The triangle model illustrated above ends with row 10. Write the totals for the following rows.

1. Row 11 _____   5. Row 15 _____   9. Row 19 _____

2. Row 12 _____   6. Row 16 _____   10. Row 20 _____

3. Row 13 _____   7. Row 17 _____   11. Row 21 _____

4. Row 14 _____   8. Row 18 _____   12. Row 22 _____

Probability and the Triangle

- If you flip 1 penny, you have 2 possible outcomes: heads or tails.
- If you flip 2 pennies at a time, you have 4 possible outcomes: (HH, HT, TH, TT).
- If you flip 3 pennies at a time, you have 8 possible outcomes.

Directions: Find this pattern on the triangle above. How many possible outcomes would you have with?

13. 4 pennies _____   16. 7 pennies _____

14. 5 pennies _____   17. 8 pennies _____

15. 6 pennies _____   18. 9 pennies _____

Brain Teaser 10

Fastest Feet

For each runner, rewrite each time in minutes and seconds.

#1	101 seconds	_____ min._____ sec.
#2	174 seconds	_____ min._____ sec.
#3	749 seconds	_____ min._____ sec.
#4	671 seconds	_____ min._____ sec.
#5	896 seconds	_____ min._____ sec.
#6	336 seconds	_____ min._____ sec.
#7	310 seconds	_____ min._____ sec.
#8	781 seconds	_____ min._____ sec.
#9	382 seconds	_____ min._____ sec.
#10	551 seconds	_____ min._____ sec.

11. Which runner had the fastest time? _____

12. Which runner had the slowest time? _____

13. Which runners took more than 10 minutes? _____

14. Which runners took less than 5 minutes? _____

Brain Teaser 11 ꙮ ꙮ ꙮ ꙮ ꙮ ꙮ ꙮ ꙮ ꙮ ꙮ ꙮ ꙮ

Arts and Crafts

Find the ending time for each class.

Class	Beginning Time	Length of Class	Ending Time
1. Macrame	11:03 A.M.	88 minutes	
2. Basket Weaving	6:34 P.M.	55 minutes	
3. Model Airplanes	6:10 P.M.	10 minutes	
4. Doll Making	9:12 A.M.	68 minutes	
5. Model Trains	1:01 P.M.	49 minutes	
6. Pottery	8:29 A.M.	45 minutes	
7. Needlepoint	10:19 A.M.	37 minutes	
8. Sewing	1:18 P.M.	51 minutes	
9. Clay Crafting	2:07 P.M.	94 minutes	
10. Leather Crafting	7:33 P.M.	48 minutes	

11. Which classes end before noon? _____

_____

12. Which classes end after noon and before 6:00 P.M.? _____

_____

13. Which classed end after 6:00 P.M.? _____

_____

Brain Teaser 12

Graphing Functions

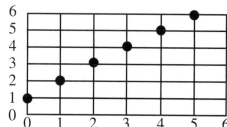

The rule for this function represented on the graph is: $f(n) = n + 1$.

Directions: Find the rule for each of these graphed functions. The first one is done for you.

1.

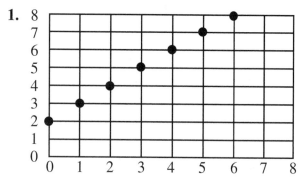

Rule: $\underline{f(n) = n + 2}$

2.

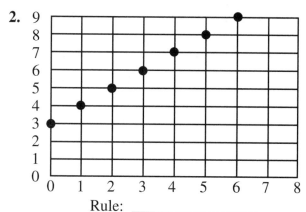

Rule: _____

3.

Rule: _____

4.

Rule: _____

5. Graph these ordered pairs on the graph below: (1, 4) (2, 6) (3, 8)

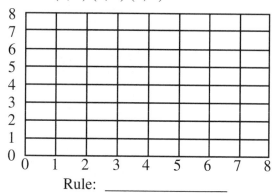

Rule: _____

6. Graph these ordered pairs on the graph below: (1, 5) (2, 6) (3, 7) (4, 8) (5, 9)

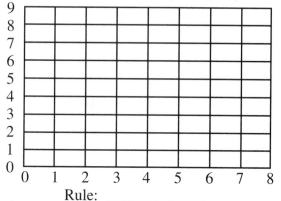

Rule: _____

Brain Teaser 13 ⟳ ⟳ ⟳ ⟳ ⟳ ⟳ ⟳ ⟳ ⟳ ⟳ ⟳

A Famous Landmark

Solve each problem. Decode the message.

1.　　A $23 + {}^-24 =$ ___	2.　　B $-97 + 1 =$ ___	3.　　E $27 - 15 =$ ___	4.　　F $58 - {}^+5 =$ ___
5.　　I $2 + {}^-87 =$ ___	6.　　L $5 + {}^-67 =$ ___	7.　　O $36 + {}^-40 =$ ___	8.　　R $40 - {}^+27 =$ ___
9.　　S $19 + 14 =$ ___	10.　　T $13 + {}^-12 =$ ___	11.　　U $43 - 28 =$ ___	12.　　Y ${}^-29 + {}^-35 =$ ___

___　___　___　___　___　___
33　　1　　⁻1　　1　　15　　42

___　___
⁻4　　7

___　___　___　___　___　___　___
⁻62　⁻85　⁻96　12　13　1　⁻64

Brain Teaser 14 ๑ ☺ ๑ ☺ ๑ ☺ ๑ ☺ ๑ ๑ ☺

Math Squares #1

Write each math problem's under the correct answer. Each row and column must equal 15.

97	400	174	
☐	☐	☐	→ 15
850	292	100	
☐	☐	☐	→ 15
1,600	240	4	
☐	☐	☐	→ 15

1. 20 x 80 = _____

2. (8 x 3) + 150 = _____

3. 149 + 143 = _____

4. 40 x 10 = _____

5. 17 x 50 = _____

6. 120 ÷ 30 = _____

7. (92 x 2) – 84 = _____

8. (48 ÷ 6) x 30 = _____

9. $9^2 + 4^2$ = _____

Brain Teaser 15

Math Squares #2

Write each math problem's number under the correct answer. Each row and column must equal 34.

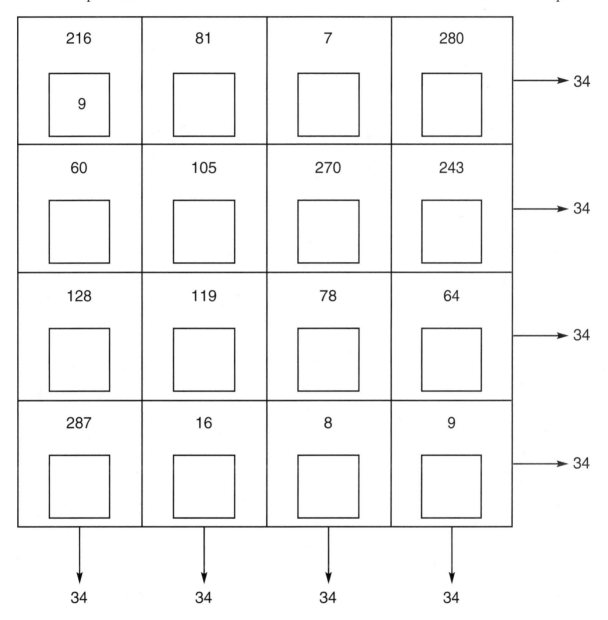

1. 4^3 = _____

2. 105 x 1 = _____

3. 56 ÷ 7 = _____

4. 28 ÷ 4 = _____

5. 16 x 8 = _____

6. 3^5 = _____

7. 48 ÷ 3 = _____

8. 41 x 7 = _____

9. 24 x 9 = _____

10. 9^2 = _____

11. 28 x 10 = _____

12. 10 x 6 = _____

13. 13 x 6 = _____

14. 9 x 30 = _____

15. 17 x 7 = _____

16. 27 ÷ 3 = _____

Brain Teaser 16

Get into Shape!

Answer each shape question.

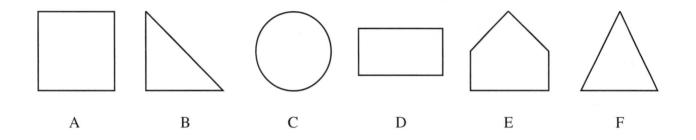

1. Which shapes have at least one right angle? _____

2. Which shape has an obtuse angle? _____

3. Which shapes have only right angles? _____

4. Which shapes have at least one acute angle? _____

5. Which shapes are triangles? _____

6. Which shapes are quadrilaterals? _____

7. Which shapes have angles that are all the same size? _____

8. Which shapes have angles that are of different sizes? _____

9. Which shapes can be divided into 5 equal sections? _____

10. Which shapes can be made using triangles of the same size? _____

Brain Teaser 17

Number Puzzle #1

Write each number in the number puzzle.

	2-Digit Numbers		3-Digit Numbers	
	13	58	103	326
	14	60	109	535
	15	72	165	696
	16	74	229	881
	18	93	314	891

Brain Teaser 18

Number Puzzle #2

Write each number in the number puzzle.

2-Digit Numbers	3-Digit Numbers	4-Digit Numbers
10	105	1,034
18	210	1,066
46	273	1,142
67	882	4,756
78	948	5,137

Brain Teaser 19

Number Puzzle #3

Write each number in the number puzzle.

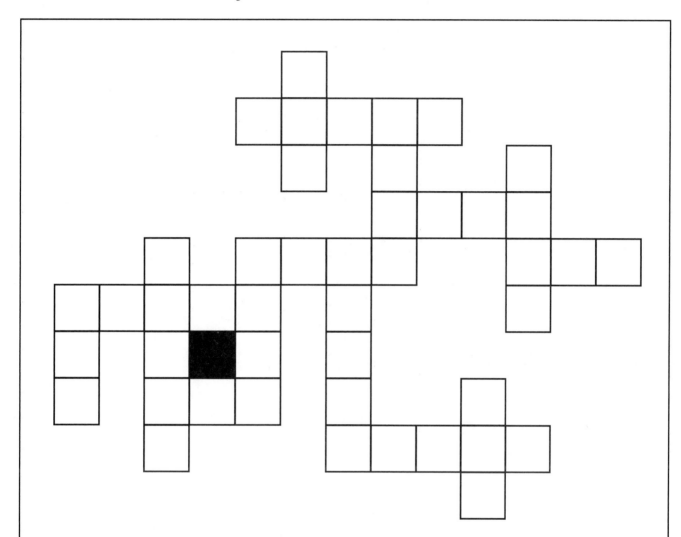

3-Digit Numbers	4-Digit Numbers	5-Digit Numbers
371	1,469	10,273
390	6,296	34,483
495	6,635	42,247
581	8,771	92,331
861	8,919	96,215

Brain Teaser 20

Number Puzzle #4

Write each number in the number puzzle.

4-Digit Numbers		5-Digit Numbers	
1,022	2,747	17,154	49,960
1,131	5,773	28,106	52,910
1,499	6,886	32,107	58,101
2,510	7,973	35,349	59,263
2,745	8,348	38,661	69,712

Brain Teaser 21 ꩜ ꩜ ꩜ ꩜ ꩜ ꩜ ꩜ ꩜ ꩜ ꩜ ꩜ ꩜ ꩜

Simple Sequences

A *sequence* is a set of numbers which follows a mathematical rule and a specific order.

Sample   Rule: multiply by 2 or *n* x 2

    (3, 6, 12, 24, 48, . . .)   Each term after the first is multiplied by 2.

Directions: Complete these sequences by filling in the blanks. Write the rule which the sequence follows. The first problem has been partially done for you.

1. (2, 4, 6, 8, 10, ____, ____, ____, ____)   Rule: _____add 2 or *n* + 2_____

2. (1, 2, 3, ____, ____, 6, 7, ____, ____)   Rule: _____

3. (9, 13, 17, ____, ____, 29, 33, ____, ____)   Rule: _____

4. (6, 14, 22, 30, ____, ____, 54, 62, ____, ____)   Rule: _____

5. (5, 10, 15, ____, ____, ____, 35, 40, ____)   Rule: _____

6. (7, 10, 13, ____, ____, 22, 25, ____, ____)   Rule: _____

7. (40, 38, 36, 34, ____, ____, ____, ____)   Rule: _____

8. (132, 121, 110, 99, ____, ____, ____, ____)   Rule: _____

9. (98, 93, 88, ____, ____, 73, 68, ____, ____)   Rule: _____

10. (4, 10, 16, ____, ____, 34, ____, 46, ____)   Rule: _____

11. (1, 2, 4, 8, ____, ____, ____, 128, ____)   Rule: _____

12. (1, 3, 9, 27, ____, ____, ____, ____)   Rule: _____

13. (3, 6, 12, ____, 48, ____, ____, ____)   Rule: _____

14. (1, 4, 16, 64, ____, ____, ____, ____)   Rule: _____

15. (5, 15, 45, ____, ____, ____, ____)   Rule: _____

16. (1, 5, 25, ____, 625, ____, ____, ____)   Rule: _____

17. (2048, ____, 512, ____, 128, ____, 32, ____)   Rule: _____

Brain Teaser 22 ぎ ❃ ♪ ❃ ♪ ❃ ♪ ❃ ♪ ❃ ♪ ❃

Harder Sequences

Some sequences involve squared numbers or cubed numbers like the example below.

    (1, 4, 9, 16, 25)   Rule: counting numbers squared

Some sequences use two operations like the example below.

    (1, 4, 13, 40, 121)   The two operations are multiply by 3 and add 1.
                            The rule can be written this way: $(n \times 3) + 1$

Directions: Study the Facts and Reminders page for this unit. Complete these sequences by filling in the blanks. Write the rule which the sequence follows.

1. (2, 5, 11, 23, _____, _____, _____, _____)   Rule: _____

2. (3, 10, 31, _____, _____, 850, _____, _____)   Rule: _____

3. (1, 6, 26, 106, _____, _____, _____, _____)   Rule: _____

4. (1, 2, 7, 32, 157, _____, _____, _____, _____)   Rule: _____

5. (1, 4, 9, _____, _____, 36, _____, _____, _____)   Rule: _____

6. (1, 8, 36, 148, _____, _____, _____, _____)   Rule: _____

7. (4, 11, 32, 95, _____, _____, _____, _____)   Rule: _____

8. (1, 5, 33, 229, _____, _____, _____, _____)   Rule: _____

9. (5, 13, 29, 61, _____, _____, _____, _____)   Rule: _____

10. (7, 15, 31, _____, 127, _____, _____, _____, _____)   Rule: _____

11. (⁻10, ⁻8, ⁻5, ⁻1, ⁺4, ⁺10, _____, _____, _____, _____)   Rule: _____

12. (27, 26, 24, 21, 17, _____, _____, ⁻1, ⁻9, ⁻18, _____)   Rule: _____

13. (100, 90, 81, 73, _____, _____, _____, _____)   Rule: _____

14. (2, 3, 5, 7, 11, 13, _____, _____, _____, _____)   Rule: _____

15. (1, 8, 27, 64, _____, _____, _____, _____)   Rule: _____

16. (⁻10, ⁻5, ⁺1, ⁺8, ⁺16, _____, _____, _____, _____)   Rule: _____

17. (⁻30, ⁻20, ⁻11, ⁻3, ⁺4, ⁺10, _____, _____, _____, _____)   Rule: _____

18. (2, 5, 10, 17, 26, _____, _____, 65, _____, _____)   Rule: _____

Brain Teaser 23 ৶ ❧ ৶ ❧ ৶ ❧ ৶ ❧ ৶ ❧ ৶ ৶ ❧

Fibonacci Sequence

The *Fibonacci sequence* is the most famous of all sequences in math. Every number after the first two 1s is computed by adding the two previous numbers.

(1, 1, 2, 3, 5, 8, 13, 21, 34, 55)   Rule: add the previous two numbers

$1 + 1 = 2$ $1 + 2 = 3$ $2 + 3 = 5$ $3 + 5 = 8$

Directions: Answer the following questions.

1. Extend the Fibonacci sequence to 20 terms.

   (1, 1, 2, 3, 5, 8, 13, 21, 34, 55, ___, ___, ___, ___, ___, ___, ___, ___, ___, ___)

2. Compute the sum of the first ten numbers in the Fibonacci sequence. _____

3. Multiply the seventh term in the sequence (13) times 11. _____
   You should get the same answer as problem #2. Double-check your work if your answers did not match.

Directions: Complete these Fibonacci sequences by filling in the blanks. Compute the sum of the first 10 terms in each sequence. Multiply the seventh term in the sequence times 11.

4. (3, 3, 6, 9, 15, ____, ____, ____, ____, ____)   Sum: _____

   Product: 11 x ____ = _____

5. (7, 7, 14, 21, 35, ____, ____, ____, ____, ____)   Sum: _____

   Product: 11 x ____ = _____

6. (10, 10, 20, 30, 50, ____, ____, ____, ____, ____)   Sum: _____

   Product: 11 x ____ = _____

7. (5, 6, 11, 17, 28, ____, ____, ____, ____, ____)   Sum: _____

   Product: 11 x ____ = _____

8. (5, 5, 10, 15, 25, ____, ____, ____, ____, ____)   Sum: _____

   Product: 11 x ____ = _____

Brain Teaser 24 ♪ ☙ ♪ ☙ ♪ ☙ ♪ ☙ ♪ ♪ ☙

Coin Combinations Less Than a Dollar

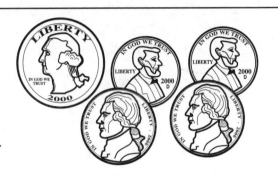

Sample

Maggie Moneytoes broke her piggy bank open and found five coins worth $0.37. Which coins did she have?

She had to have two pennies. The only combination of three coins worth $0.35 is one quarter and two nickels.

Directions: Make a chart to solve each of these problems. Use another piece of paper, if necessary.

1. Festus Flattbroke found five coins worth $0.57 in his shirt pocket. Which coins did he find?

Number of Coins	Amount of Money
2 pennies	$0.02
Totals: 5 coins	$0.57

2. Johnny Cashless found 17 coins worth $0.21 under the couch. Which coins did he find?

Number of Coins	Amount of Money
Totals: 17 coins	$0.21

3. Mr. Monnebaggs cracked his piggy bank and found six coins worth $0.96. He did not have a half dollar. What coins did he find?

4. Mrs. Monnebaggs opened her piggy bank and found five coins worth $0.22. What coins did she find?

5. Bertha Biggspender found seven coins worth $0.39 in her pencil box. Which coins did she find?

6. You opened your piggy bank and found five coins worth $0.78. Which coins did you find?

Money

Brain Teaser 25 ꙮ

Coin Combinations More Than a Dollar

	Number of Coins	Amount of Money
Festus Flattbroke found nine coins worth $1.23 under his bed. None of the coins was a half dollar. Which coins did he find?	3 pennies	$0.03
	4 quarters	$1.00
	2 dimes	$0.20
Totals:	9 coins	$1.23

Facts

- At least three of the coins must be pennies.
- There were no half dollars so the dollar can be four quarters.
- The remaining $0.20 must be two dimes.

Directions: Make a chart to solve each of these problems. Use another piece of paper, if necessary.

1. Sondra Sorich opened her piggy bank so she could go to the mall. She found 11 coins worth $2.11. What coins did she have?

2. Bertha Biggspender found 13 coins worth $3.03 in her makeup bag. She did not have any dimes. Which coins did she find?

3. Maggie Moneytoes found 20 coins worth $3.27 in her shoe. She did not have any nickels. Which coins did she find?

4. Johnny Cashless kept his money in an old sock. He had 19 coins worth $4.51. He did not have a half dollar. Which coins did he have?

5. Mr. Monnebaggs had 14 coins worth $3.97 in his office safe. He did not have any dimes. Which coins did he have?

6. Mrs. Monnebaggs found 13 coins worth $4.14 in her hat. She did not have any nickels. Which coins did she have?

7. You found 27 coins worth $1.17 in an old box. There were no nickels. Which coins did you find?

8. Your best friend found 37 coins worth $7.30 in an old coin purse. There were no half dollars and only one dime. Which coins did your friend find?

Brain Teaser 26 ꙮ ꙮ ꙮ ꙮ ꙮ ꙮ ꙮ ꙮ ꙮ ꙮ ꙮ ꙮ

Coin Combinations and Dollar Bills

Bertha Biggspender had $7.51 in her purse. She had 3 dollar bills and 19 coins. Which coins did she have?

	Number of Coins	Amount of Money
	1 penny	$0.01
	18 quarters	$4.50
Totals:	19 coins	$4.51
	3 dollar bills	$3.00
		$7.51

Remember the following:

- Make a chart.
- Do pennies first.
- Do not forget half dollars.
- Match exact amount of money.
- Match exact number of coins and bills.

Directions: Make a chart to solve each of these problems. Use another piece of paper, if necessary.

1. Festus Flattbroke had exactly $9.37 in his pocket. He had 4 dollar bills and 26 coins with only 1 nickel. Which coins did he have?

2. Bertha Biggspender found a stash of money in her desk. She had $9.49. She had 5 dollar bills and 54 coins, but no coins were larger than a dime. What coins did she have?

3. Your mother found a cookie jar full of coins about which she had forgotten. She counted 96 coins worth $21.55. She had no half dollars and only 1 nickel. Which coins did she have?

4. Your best friend broke open her piggy bank which had $30.59. She had 1 five dollar bill, 2 dollar bills, 4 half dollars, and no nickels. She had a total of 108 coins. Which coins did she have?

5. Johnny Cashless had $10.00 in his sock. He had 1 dollar bill, 1 dime, and no half dollars. He had 43 coins. Which coins did he have?

6. Mister Monnebaggs found a sack of money in his closet worth $49.65 with 1 dollar bill, 3 nickels, and 1 half dollar. He had a total of 244 coins. What coins did he have?

7. Maggie Moneytoes found a sack of cash worth $38.66 in her boot. There was 1 ten dollar bill, 1 five dollar bill, and 3 one dollar bills. She had a total of 100 coins with no half dollars and only 1 nickel. What coins did she have?

8. The fourth grade teacher found $4.78 under her car seat. She had 1 dollar bill and 38 coins. There were no half dollars. She had exactly twice as many dimes as nickels and twice as many nickels as quarters. What coins did she find?

Brain Teaser 27

A Roll of the Dice #1

Add the appropriate signs (+, −, x, ÷) to complete each math problem. (Each sign is used one time in each math problem.) Solve each problem going from left to right.

1.   7 ☐ 8 ☐ 9 ☐ 3 ☐ 5 [=]   40

2.   4 ☐ 2 ☐ 1 [x] 18 ☐ 20 [=]   38

3.   9 ☐ 10 [÷] 9 ☐ 14 ☐ 6 [=]   18

4.   36 [+] 24 ☐ 0 ☐ 2 ☐ 30 [=]   900

5.   42 [−] 6 ☐ 2 ☐ 30 ☐ 3 [=]   34

6.   35 [x] 4 ☐ 67 ☐ 9 ☐ 16 [=]   7

7.   76 ☐ 4 [+] 62 ☐ 9 ☐ 194 [=]   535

8.   47 [x] 8 ☐ 124 ☐ 250 ☐ 50 [=]   5

9.   91 ☐ 49 ☐ 88 [÷] 4 ☐ 41 [=]   533

Brain Teaser 28 ᗧ ᗣ ᗧ ᗣ ᗧ ᗣ ᗧ ᗣ ᗧ ᗣ ᗧ ᗣ ᗧ

A Roll of the Dice #2

Add the appropriate signs (+, −, x, ÷) to complete each math problem. (Each sign is used one time in each math problem.) Solve each problem going from left to right.

1. 187 [−] 91 [ ] 8 [ ] 6 [ ] 3 [=] _75_

2. 210 [ ] 4 [+] 105 [ ] 45 [ ] 30 [=] _30_

3. 96 [ ] 24 [ ] 13 [ ] 105 [x] 3 [=] _366_

4. 64 [ ] 4 [ ] 8 [ ] 105 [+] 110 [=] _133_

5. 104 [−] 33 [ ] 61 [ ] 4 [ ] 8 [=] _66_

6. 64 [ ] 77 [ ] 3 [x] 9 [ ] 99 [=] _324_

7. 76 [ ] 4 [+] 84 [ ] 2 [ ] 194 [=] _0_

8. 77 [ ] 12 [ ] 6 [ ] 10 [+] 31 [=] _70_

9. 47 [ ] 109 [−] 83 [ ] 6 [ ] 6 [=] _73_

Brain Teaser 29 ⟍ ⟍ ⟍ ⟍ ⟍ ⟍ ⟍ ⟍ ⟍ ⟍ ⟍ ⟍

Who's the Smartest?

Logic problems can often be solved by making a simple chart or a drawing. Solve the problem sentence by sentence.

Sample

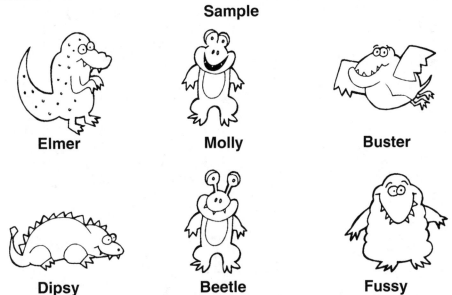

Elmer   Molly   Buster

Dipsy   Beetle   Fussy

Dipsy is smarter than Beetle but not as smart as Elmer. Molly is smarter than Elmer but not as smart as Fussy. Buster is not as smart as Beetle. Who is the smartest of them all? Who is the least smart?

Start with the first sentence: Dipsy is smarter than Beetle but not as smart as Elmer. Make a chart like this:

(less smart) ←———+———————————+———————————+———→ (smarter)
                Beetle   Dipsy   Elmer

Do the second sentence: Molly is smarter than Elmer but not as smart as Fussy. Fill in the names on the chart to show that Fussy is smarter than Molly and Molly is smarter than Elmer.

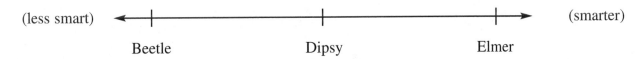

(less smart) ←——+———————+———————+———————+———————+——→ (smarter)
              Beetle   Dipsy   Elmer   Molly   Fussy

Do the third sentence: Buster is not as smart as Beetle. Complete the chart.

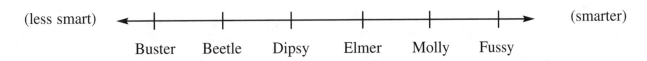

(less smart) ←——+———————+———————+———————+———————+——→ (smarter)
              Buster Beetle Dipsy   Elmer   Molly   Fussy

Brain Teaser 29 *(cont.)* ᵔ ᕙ ᵔ ᕙ ᵔ ᕙ ᵔ ᕙ ᵔ ᕙ

Who's the Smartest? *(cont.)*

Directions: Fill out the chart to help find the answers to the questions.

1. Nick is smarter than Curly but not nearly as smart as Nosey. Daisy is smarter than Nosey but not as smart as Mickey. Slick is smarter than Mickey.

    Who is the least smart? _____ Who is the smartest? _____

    (less smart) ⬅———————————————————➡ (smarter)

    _____ _____ _____ _____ _____ _____

2. Rocket is smarter than Fussy but not as smart as Doc. Molly is smarter than Doc but not as smart as you are. Buster is not as smart as Fussy.

    Who is the least smart? _____ Who is the smartest? _____

    (less smart) ⬅———————————————————➡ (smarter)

    _____ _____ _____ _____ _____ _____

3. Daisy has more teeth than Dipsy and Beetle but not as many teeth as Curly. Nick has more teeth than Beetle but not as many teeth as Dipsy. Elmer has fewer teeth than Beetle. Buster has more teeth than Curly.

    Who has the fewest teeth? _____ Who has the most teeth? _____

    (fewest) ⬅———————————————————➡ (most)

    _____ _____ _____ _____ _____ _____ _____

    Buster has 7 teeth. How many teeth does each person have?

    Elmer: _____ tooth   Daisy: _____ teeth

    Beetle: _____ teeth   Curly: _____ teeth

    Nick: _____ teeth   Buster: _____ teeth

    Dipsy: _____ teeth

Brain Teaser 30 ꩜ ꩜ ꩜ ꩜ ꩜ ꩜ ꩜ ꩜ ꩜ ꩜ ꩜

Logic Problems and Charts

Directions: Use the method you previously learned to solve each of these problems.

1. Buster weighs 40 pounds more than Rocket and 80 pounds less than Molly. Daisy weighs 100 pounds more than Molly. Curly weighs 60 pounds less than Rocket.

   Who weighs the least? _____ Who weighs the most? _____

   (least) ⟵————————————————————————————⟶ (most)

   _____ _____ _____ _____ _____

   Buster weighs 200 pounds. How much does each weigh?

   Buster: ___200___ pounds   Curly: _____ pounds

   Molly: _____ pounds   Rocket: _____ pounds

   Daisy: _____ pounds

2. Lanky is 8 centimeters taller than Elmer, but he is 6 centimeters shorter than Molly. Buster is 9 centimeters taller than Molly but 10 centimeters shorter than Hairy. Nosey is 10 centimeters taller than Hairy. Dipsy is 5 centimeters shorter than Elmer.

   Who is the shortest? _____ Who is the tallest? _____

   (shortest) ⟵————————————————————————————⟶ (tallest)

   _____ _____ _____ _____ _____ _____ _____

   Dipsy is 120 centimeters tall. How tall is each person?

   Dipsy: _____ cm   Buster: _____ cm

   Lanky: _____ cm   Hairy: _____ cm

   Elmer: _____ cm   Nosey: _____ cm

   Molly: _____ cm

3. Buster has a longer nose than Lanky, but his nose is not as long as Hairy's. Elmer has a longer nose than Hairy, but it is not as long as Dipsy's nose. Nosey has a longer nose than Dipsy's. Dandy has the longest nose of all. On the back of this paper, make a chart showing the length of noses from shortest to longest.

Brain Teaser 30 (cont.) ⊃ ☺ ⊃ ☺ ⊃ ☺ ⊃ ⊃ ☺

Logic Problems and Charts (cont.)

Directions: Make a chart to help you solve these problems. Work step by step.

1. Daisy has twice as much money as Rocket and exactly half as much as Dipsy. Fussy has twice as much money as Dipsy. Daisy has $100. How much money does each individual have?

   _____Daisy_____ ___$100___ _____ _____

   _____ _____ _____ _____

2. Buster is one year older than Molly and two years younger than Beetle. Nick is one year older than Beetle and one year younger than Doc. Doc is one year younger than Mickey and two years younger than Rocket. Curly is two years older than Rocket.

   Who is the youngest? _____ Who is the oldest? _____

   Buster is six years old. How old is each individual?

   _____ _____ years old   _____ _____ years old

   ___Buster___ ___6___ years old   _____ _____ years old

   _____ _____ years old   _____ _____ years old

   _____ _____ years old   _____ _____ years old

3. Every day Dipsy eats four times as much as Elmer but only half as much as Molly. Daisy eats four times as much as food as Molly but only half as much as Buster. Elmer eats four times as much as Beetle. Curly eats only half as much as Beetle. Mickey eats two times as much as Buster.

   Who eats the least? _____ Who eats the most? _____

   Elmer eats 10 pounds of food. How many pounds of food does each individual eat?

   _____ _____ lbs.   _____ _____ lbs.

   _____ _____ lbs.   _____ _____ lbs.

   ___Elmer___ ___10___ lbs.   _____ _____ lbs.

   _____ _____ lbs.   _____ _____ lbs.

Brain Teaser 31 ⊚ ⊙ ⊚ ⊙ ⊚ ⊙ ⊚ ⊙ ⊚ ⊙ ⊚ ⊙

TV Channels

For problems 1–10, solve each math problem. Then read each clue to find the channel for each television program to problems 11–20. Be careful—some of the clues might seem to fit two different television programs—but they don't!

1. $(41 + 67) \div 4 =$ _____

2. $(38 - 25) \times 10 =$ _____

3. $(48 \div 12) + 57 =$ _____

4. $(64 \times 11) - 289 =$ _____

5. $(36 + 65) \div 3 =$ _____

6. $(28 - 14) \times 54 =$ _____

7. $(96 \div 12) + 91 =$ _____

8. $(26 \times 10) - 153 =$ _____

9. $(78 + 63) \div 3 =$ _____

10. $(54 - 39) \times 8 =$ _____

11. *Life with the Twins* is on a channel divisible only by 5 and 83.

    It is on channel _____.

12. *Tulare Public* is on a channel divisible by 11.

    It is on channel _____.

13. *About the Town* is on channel $8^2 - 3$.

    It is on channel _____.

14. *Nightly News* is on channel 3^3.

    It is on channel _____.

15. *When in Oregon* is on channel $5^3 - 18$.

    It is on channel _____.

16. *Guess Who?* is on a channel that is a multiple of 13.

    It is on channel _____.

17. *Three in a Row* is on an odd numbered channel between 0 and 100.

    It is on channel _____.

18. *20 Questions* is on a channel divisible by 18.

    It is on channel _____.

19. *Hot Seat!* is on an even numbered channel.

    It is on channel _____.

20. *Power Play* is on a channel that is a multiple of 12.

    It is on channel _____.

Brain Teaser 32 ◗ ❂ ◗ ❂ ◗ ❂ ◗ ❂ ◗ ❂ ◗ ❂

Number Teaser #1

Write the multiplication problem for each one of the clues to find the mystery number.

_____ x _____ = 56	_____ x _____ = 30	_____ x _____ = 13	_____ x _____ = 24
_____ x _____ = 38	_____ x _____ = 77	_____ x _____ = 4	_____ x _____ = 54
_____ x _____ = 33	_____ x _____ = 65	_____ x _____ = 87	_____ x _____ = 15
_____ x _____ = 22	_____ x _____ = 72	_____ x _____ = 12	_____ x _____ = 48

1. Products with 10 as a factor.

2. Products with 9 as a factor.

3. Products with 8 as a factor.

4. Products with 7 as a factor.

5. Products with 6 as a factor.

6. Products with 5 as a factor.

7. Products with 4 as a factor.

8. Products with 3 as a factor.

9. Products with 2 as a factor.

10. What is the mystery number?_____

Number Teaser #2

Follow the clues to find the mystery number.

1,281,096	232,398	669,761	941,093
136,777	410,415	842,151	951,010
161,918	613,124	854,721	953,688
225,579	641,438	883,934	976,143

1. Cross off the numbers that can be evenly divided by 3.

2. Cross off the numbers that have the same number of odd and even digits.

3. Cross off the numbers that are even.

4. Cross off the numbers that have the greatest number of odd digits.

5. What is the mystery number? _____

Brain Teaser 33 ᵔ ☜ ᵔ ☜ ᵔ ☜ ᵔ ☜ ᵔ ☜ ᵔ ᵔ ☜

Number Teaser #3

Follow the clues to find the mystery number.

18	52	28	32
84	92	95	10
36	96	64	70
45	63	50	84

1. Cross off the numbers evenly divided by both 2 and 4.

2. Cross off the numbers evenly divided by 3 and 6.

3. Cross off the numbers evenly divided by 3 and 9.

4. Cross off the numbers evenly divided by 5 and 10.

5. What is the mystery number?

   _____

Number Teaser #4

Follow the clues to find the mystery number.

1,281,096	4,410,933	5,556,169	8,276,935
1,886,807	4,486,864	6,485,101	8,945,532
1,942,781	4,726,783	6,752,022	9,108,106
3,100,014	5,125,536	7,370,429	9,492,784

1. Cross of the numbers that have two of the same digit in a row.

2. Cross off the numbers that have three of the same digit in a row.

3. Cross off the numbers that have the same digit used exactly twice in the number.

4. What is the mystery number? _____

Brain Teaser 34

Number Puzzle 24

Arrange the numbers in each puzzle so that . . .

- Each number is used only one time in each row and column. (Each number will be used 4 times in the puzzle.)

- Each row, column, and diagonal make the final product. (*Hint:* Write the numbers on sticky notes and use the notes to solve the puzzle.)

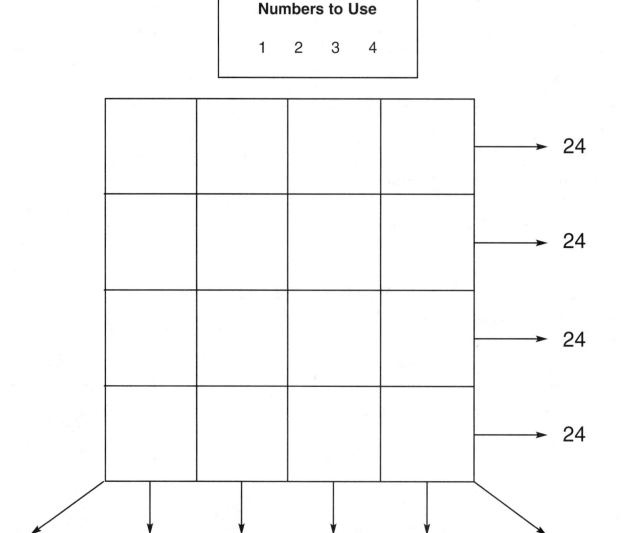

Brain Teaser 35

Name the President

Which president's picture is on the $100,000 bill? Solve each problem by rounding to the nearest cent and decode the answer.

1.　　**D** $38.89 x .13	2.　　**I** $78.47 x .29	3.　　**L** $21.03 x .93	4.　　**N** $72.41 x .16
5.　　**O** $56.10 x .54	6.　　**R** $68.58 x .47	7.　　**S** $10.27 x .59	8.　　**W** $29.58 x .11

——————　——————　——————　——————　——————　——————　——————

$3.25　　$30.29　　$30.29　　$5.06　　$32.23　　$30.29　　$3.25

——————　——————　——————　——————　——————　——————

$3.25　　$22.76　　$19.56　　$6.06　　$30.29　　$11.59

Answer Key

Pages 4 and 5

1. a. $d + 5$
   b. $d + d + 5$ or $2d + 5$
2. a. $2w = (w + 4) + 3$
   b. $2(w + 4) = (3w + 1)$
   c. $2w + 2(w + 4) = 36$
3. $n + n + 10 = 50$
   $n = 20$ inches
4. $n + 5 + n = 35$
   $n = 15$ votes; $5 + n = 20$ votes for Ian
5. $n + 2n < 27$; $n < 9$
6. $n + n + 1 + n + 2 = 123$; $3n + 3 = 123$; $n = 40$; the numbers are 40, 41, and 42
7. $x + 16 = 2x$
   Father = 48 years
   son = 16 years
8. $n + 5 = 14$
   $n = 9$ years old
9. $n - 4 = 10$
   $n = 14$ years old
10. $x + 7 = 20$
    $x = 13$ years old
11. $x - 10 = 3$
    $x = 13$ years old
12. $1 + 2n = 19$
    $n = 9$ years old
13. let x = Gloria's contribution
    $\$30.00 + \$10.00 = \$40.00$; $\$40.00 + x = \$54.99$ so $x = \$14.99$
14. let x = total number of bags
    $5x + 2x = 7$; $7x = 252$; $x = 36$ bags
15. $270 + (150 + x) + x = 800$; $420 + 2x = 800$; $x = 190$ seats; if there are 190 seats in Theatre 3, then Theatre 2 has $150 + 190 = 340$ seats
16. $2n + 13 = 75$
    Add (-13) to both sides.
    $2n = 62$
    Divide both sides by 2.
    $n = 31$

17. $x + (2x + 1) = 16$
    $x = 5$ feet
    $2x + 1 = 11$ feet
18. $x + (x + 1) + (x + 2) = 69$
    $x = 22$
    $x + 1 = 23$
    $x + 2 = 24$
19. $9x + 2x = 22$
    $x = 12$
    4 gallons yellow
    18 gallons white
20. $(\$8 \times 40) + .15(\$50x) = \$470$
    $\$320 + \$7.5x = \$470$
    $- \$320 \qquad = - \$320$
    _____
    $\$7.5x = \$150$
    $x = 20$ bottles

Page 6

	9	18	36	72
Brenda	X	X	X	O
Casey	X	X	O	X
Daniel	O	X	X	X
Eden	X	O	X	X

Brenda received 72 cracked or broken eggs.
Casey received 36 cracked or broken eggs.
Daniel received 9 cracked or broken eggs.
Eden received 18 cracked or broken eggs.

Page 7

	25	31	34	71	84
Connor	X	O	X	X	X
Hannah	X	X	X	O	X
Logan	X	X	X	X	X
Stan	X	X	O	X	X
Tara	X	X	X	X	O

Connor's number is 31.
Hannah's number is 71.
Logan's number is 25.
Stan's number is 34.
Tara's number is 84.

Page 9

Scuby Diving

Page 10

	318-1041	528-6321	796-9934	837-2107	844-1109
Bella	X	X	X	O	X
Destiny	X	X	O	X	X
Ky	X	X	X	X	O
Kendra	O	X	X	X	X
Ryder	X	O	X	X	X

Bella's number is 318-1041.
Destiny's number is 796-9934.
Ryder's number is 528-6321.
Ky's number is 844-1109.
Kendra's number is 837-2107.

Page 11

	50%	55%	75%	80%	85%	100%
Andrew	X	X	O	X	X	X
Brian	X	X	X	O	X	X
Charles	X	X	X	X	O	X
Emily	X	O	X	X	X	X
Molly	O	X	X	X	X	X
Sheila	X	X	X	X	X	O

Andrew's score was 75%.
Brian's score was 80%.
Charles' score was 85%.
Emily's score was 55%.
Emily's score was 55%.
Sheila's score was 100%.

Page 12

	Camelot Park	Hyde park	Park Place	Park West	391	547	1,062	1,079
Bud	X	X	X	O	O	X	X	X
Helen	X	O	X	X	X	X	X	O
Jodie	X	X	O	X	X	O	X	X
Nick	O	X	X	X	X	X	O	X

Bud delivers 391 newspapers to the residents of Park West.
Helen delivers 1,079 newspapers to the residents of Hyde Park.
Nick delivers 1,062 newspapers to the residents of Camelot Park.
Jodie delivers 597 newspapers to the residents of Park Place.

Page 14

1. 1 trillion
2. 1 quadrillion
3. 1 quintillion
4. 1 sextillion
5. 1 septillion
6. 1 octillion
7. 1 trillion
8. 1 quadrillion
9. 1 quintillion
10. 1 sextillion
11. 1,000,000,000,000
12. 1,000,000,000,000,000
13. 1,000,000,000,000,000,000
14. 1,000,000,000,000,000,000,000
15. 1,000,000,000,000
16. 1,000,000,000,000,000,000
17. 1,000,000,000
18. 1,000,000,000
19. 25,000,000,000,000,000
20. 81,000,000,000,000,000,000

Page 16

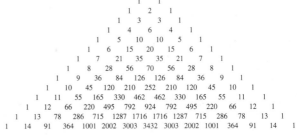

Row 9: 126, 126
Row 10: 252
Row 11: 462, 462
Row 12: 924
Row 13: 1716, 1716
Row 14: 3432

2. 1
3. second line in
4. 1, 15, 105, 455, 1365, 3003, 5005, 6435, 6435, 5005, 3003, 1365, 455, 105, 15, 1

Answer Key (cont.)

Page 17

Top: 1, 2, 4, 8, 16, 32, 64, 128, 256, 512, 1024; the total is doubled

1. 2,048
2. 4,096
3. 8,192
4. 16,384
5. 32,768
6. 65,536
7. 131,072
8. 262,144
9. 524,288
10. 1,048,576
11. 2,097,152
12. 4,194,304
13. 16
14. 32
15. 64
16. 128
17. 256
18. 512

Page 18

1. 1 min. 41 sec.
2. 2 min. 54 sec.
3. 12 min. 29 sec.
4. 11 min. 11 sec.
5. 14 min. 56 sec.
6. 5 min. 36 sec.
7. 5 min. 10 sec.
8. 13 min. 1 sec.
9. 6 min. 22 sec.
10. 9 min. 11 sec.
11. #1
12. #5
13. #3, #4, #5, #8
14. #1, #2

Page 19

1. 12:31 P.M.
2. 7:29 P.M.
3. 6:20 P.M.
4. 10:20 P.M.
5. 1:50 P.M.
6. 9:14 A.M.
7. 10:56 A.M.
8. 2:09 P.M.
9. 3:41 P.M.
10. 8:21 P.M.

11. Doll Making, Pottery, Needlepoint
12. Macrame, Model Trains, Sewing, Clay Crafting
13. Basket Weaving, Model Airplanes, Leather Crafting

Page 20

1. $f(n) = n + 2$
2. $f(n) = n + 3$
3. $f(n) = n + 1$
4. $f(n) = n + 4$
5. $f(n) = (n \times 2) + 2$
6. $f(n) = n + 4$

Page 21

Statue of Liberty

Page 22

top row: 9, 4, 2
middle row: 5, 3, 7
bottom row: 1, 8, 6

1. 1,600
2. 174
3. 292
4. 400
5. 850
6. 4
7. 100
8. 240
9. 97

Page 23

top row: 9, 10, 4, 11
second row: 12, 2, 14, 6
third row: 5, 15, 13, 1
bottom row: 8, 7, 3, 16

1. 64
2. 105
3. 8
4. 7
5. 128
6. 243
7. 16
8. 287
9. 216
10. 81
11. 280
12. 60
13. 78
14. 270
15. 119
16. 9

Page 24

1. A, B, D, E
2. E
3. A, D
4. B, F
5. B, F
6. A, D
7. A, D, F
8. B, E
9. A, C, D, E
10. A, B, D, E, F

Page 25

Page 26

Page 27

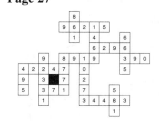

Page 28

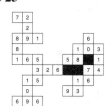

Page 29

1. (2, 4, 6, 8, 10, 12, 14, 16, 18); $n + 2$
2. (1, 2, 3, 4, 5, 6, 7, 8, 9); $n + 1$
3. (9, 13, 17, 21, 25, 29, 33, 37, 41); $n + 4$
4. (6, 14, 22, 30, 38, 46, 54, 62, 70, 78); $n + 8$
5. (5, 10, 15, 20, 25, 30, 35, 40, 45); $n + 5$
6. (7, 10, 13, 16, 19, 22, 25, 28, 31); $n + 3$
7. (40, 38, 36, 34, 32, 30, 28, 26); $n - 2$
8. (132, 121, 110, 99, 88, 77, 66, 55); $n - 11$
9. (98, 93, 88, 83, 78, 73, 68, 63, 58); $n - 5$
10. (4, 10, 16, 22, 28, 34, 40, 46, 52); $n + 6$
11. (1, 2, 4, 8, 16, 32, 64, 128, 256); $n \times 2$
12. (1, 3, 9, 27, 81, 243, 729, 2187); $n \times 3$
13. (3, 6, 12, 24, 48, 96, 192, 384); $n \times 2$
14. (1, 4, 16, 64, 256, 1024, 4096, 16384); $n \times 4$
15. (5, 15, 45, 135, 405, 1215, 3645); $n \times 3$
16. (1, 5, 25, 125, 625, 3125, 15625, 78125); $n \times 5$
17. (2048, 1024, 512, 256, 128, 64, 32, 16); $n \div 2$

Page 30

1. (2, 5, 11, 23, 47, 95, 191, 383); $(n \times 2) + 1$
2. (3, 10, 31, 94, 283, 850, 2551, 7654); $(n \times 3) + 1$
3. (1, 6, 26, 106, 426, 1706, 6826, 27306); $(n \times 4) + 2$
4. (1, 2, 7, 32, 157, 782, 3907, 19532, 97657); $(n \times 5) - 3$
5. (1, 4, 9, 16, 25, 36, 49, 64, 81); counting numbers squared
6. (1, 8, 36, 148, 596, 2388, 9556, 38228); $(n \times 4) + 4$
7. (4, 11, 32, 95, 284, 851, 2552, 7655); $(n \times 3) - 1$
8. (1, 5, 33, 229, 1601, 11205, 78433, 549029); $(n \times 7) - 2$
9. (5, 13, 29, 61, 125, 253, 509, 1021, 2045); $(n \times 2) + 3$
10. (7, 15, 31, 63, 127, 255, 511, 1023, 2047); $(n \times 2) + 1$

Answer Key (cont.)

11. (⁻10, ⁻8, ⁻5, ⁻1, ⁺4, ⁺10, ⁺17, ⁺25, ⁺34, ⁺44); add ⁺2, ⁺3, ⁺4, etc.
12. (27, 26, 24, 21, 17, 12, 6, ⁻1, ⁻9, ⁻18, ⁻28); subtract 1, 2, 3, etc.
13. (100, 90, 81, 73, 66, 60, 55, 51); subtract 10, 9, 8, etc.
14. (2, 3, 5, 7, 11, 13, 17, 19, 23, 29); prime numbers
15. (1, 8, 27, 64, 125, 216, 343, 512); counting numbers cubed
16. (⁻10, ⁻5, ⁺1, ⁺8, ⁺16, ⁺25, ⁺35, ⁺46, ⁺58); add ⁺5, ⁺6, ⁺7, etc.
17. (⁻30, ⁻20, ⁻11, ⁻3, ⁺4, ⁺10, ⁺15, ⁺19, ⁺22, ⁺24); add ⁺10, ⁺9, ⁺8, etc.
18. (2, 5, 10, 17, 26, 37, 50, 65, 82, 101); counting numbers squared + 1

Page 31
1. (89, 144, 233, 377, 610, 987, 1597, 2584, 4181, 6765)
2. 143
3. 143
4. (24, 39, 63, 102, 165) sum: 429 product: 11 x 39 = 429
5. (56, 91, 147, 238, 385) sum: 1001 product 11 x 91 = 1001
6. (80, 130, 210, 340, 550) sum: 1430 product 11 x 130 = 1430
7. (45, 73, 118, 191, 309) sum: 803 product: 11 x 73 = 803
8. (40, 65, 105, 170, 275) sum: 715 product: 11 x 65 = 715
9. Answers will vary.

Page 32
1. 2 pennies, 1 nickel, 2 quarters
2. 16 pennies, 1 nickel

3. 1 penny, 2 dimes, 3 quarters
4. 2 pennies, 2 nickels, 1 dime
5. 4 pennies, 2 nickels, 1 quarter
6. 3 pennies, 1 quarter, 1 half dollar

Page 33
1. 1 penny, 2 nickels, 8 quarters or 1 penny, 1 half dollar, 5 quarters, 3 dimes, 1 nickel
2. 3 pennies, 8 quarters, 2 half dollars
3. 2 pennies, 10 dimes, 7 quarters, 1 half dollar
4. 1 penny, 18 quarters
5. 2 pennies, 4 nickels, 1 quarter, 7 half dollars
6. 4 pennies, 1 dime, 8 half dollars
7. 10 dimes, 17 pennies
8. 28 quarters, 1 dime, 3 nickels, 5 pennies

Page 34
1. 20 quarters, 2 pennies, 1 nickel, 3 dimes
2. 39 dimes, 11 nickels, 4 pennies
3. 80 quarters, 15 dimes, 1 nickel
4. 4 half dollars, 9 pennies, 15 dimes, 80 quarters
5. 1 dime, 34 quarters, 8 nickels
6. 3 nickels, 1 half dollar, 160 quarters, 80 dimes,
7. 72 quarters, 26 dimes, 1 nickel, 1 penny
8. 3 pennies, 20 dimes, 10 nickels, 5 quarters

Page 35
1. +, x, ÷, −
2. −, ÷, x, +
3. x, ÷, +, −
4. +, −, ÷, x
5. −, x, +, ÷
6. x, +, ÷, −

7. ÷, +, x, −
8. x, −, −, ÷
9. +, −, ÷, x

Page 36
1. −, ÷, x, +
2. x, +, −, ÷
3. ÷, +, +, x
4. ÷, x, −, +
5. −, +, x, ÷
6. +, ÷, x, −
7. x, +, +, −
8. −, x, ÷, +
9. +, −, x, ÷

Page 38
1. least smart: Curly smartest: Slick
2. least smart: Buster smartest: You
3. fewest teeth: Elmer most teeth: Buster
   Elmer – 1 tooth
   Beetle – 2 teeth
   Nick – 3 teeth
   Dipsy – 4 teeth
   Curly – 6 teeth
   Buster – 7 teeth

Page 39
1. weighs the least: Curly weighs the most: Daisy
   Curly – 100 pounds
   Rocket – 160 pounds
   Buster – 200 pounds
   Molly – 280 pounds
   Daisy – 380 pounds
2. shortest: Dipsy tallest: Nosey
   Dipsy – 120 cm
   Elmer – 125 cm
   Lanky – 133 cm
   Molly – 139 cm
   Buster – 148 cm
   Hairy – 158 cm
   Nosey – 168 cm
3. Lanky, Buster, Hairy, Elmer, Dipsy, Nosey, Dandy

Page 40
1. Rocket $50; Daisy $100; Dipsy $200; Fussy $400

2. youngest: Molly oldest: Curly
   Molly – 5; Buster – 6;
   Beetle – 8; Nick – 9;
   Doc – 10; Mickey – 11;
   Rocket – 12; Curly – 14
3. eats the least: Curly eats the most: Mickey
   Curly – 1.25
   Beetle – 2.5
   Elmer – 10
   Dipsy – 40
   Molly – 80
   Daisy – 320
   Buster – 640
   Mickey – 1280

Page 41
1. 27
2. 130
3. 61
4. 415
5. 34
6. 756
7. 99
8. 107
9. 47
10. 120
11. 415
12. 99
13. 61
14. 27
15. 107
16. 130
17. 47
18. 756
19. 34
20. 120

Page 42
Number Teaser #1
The mystery number is 13
Number Teaser #2
The mystery number is 941,093.

Page 43
Number Teaser #3
The mystery number is 95.
Number Teaser #4
The mystery number is 8,276,935.

Page 44
sample answer
top row: 4, 3, 1, 2
second row: 2, 1, 3, 4
third row: 3, 4, 2, 1
bottom row: 1, 2, 4, 3

Page 45
1. $5.06
2. $22.76
3. $19.56
4. $11.59
5. $30.29
6. $32.23
7. $6.06
8. $3.25
Secret Message:
Woodrow Wilson